NEW
LIFE

All Work that Begins Ends

Edward Stone Gleason

A woman was carrying a jar full of meal. While she was walking along a distant road, the handle of the jar broke and the meal spilled behind her along the road. She didn't know it; she hadn't noticed a problem. When she reached her house, she put the jar down and discovered that it was empty.

— THE GOSPEL ACCORDING TO THOMAS

~

Though a little one, the master word looms large in meaning. It is the open sesame to every portal, the great equalizer in the world, the true philosopher's stone which transmutes the base metal of humanity into gold. The stupid man among you it will make bright, the bright man brilliant, and the brilliant steady. With the master word in your heart all things are possible, and without it all study is vanity and vexation. The miracles of life are with it; the blind see by touch, the deaf hear with eyes, the dumb speak with fingers. To the youth it brings hope, to the middle-aged confidence, to the aged repose. True balm of hurt minds, in its presence the heart of the sorrowful is lightened and consoled... And the master word is work, *a little one, but fraught with momentous consequences if you can but write it on the tables of your heart and bind it upon your forehead.*

—Sir William Osler

TABLE OF CONTENTS

Everything that Begins Ends

Everything that begins ends. Death happens. Nothing—no person, no job, no friendship, no institution—is forever. We all know this; nonetheless, we live most of our lives in denial, which is folly.

But there is more, much more. This conviction continues and concludes: Every ending contains the promise of a new beginning.

Life is driven by renewal, the persistent energy of rebirth that makes all things new. Pain and loss and death are inevitable, but each and every time they happen, there will be new life. Death happens, but it is never the final answer.

Everything that begins ends, and every ending contains the promise of a new beginning.

This conviction makes human life possible and new life a reality.

What Is NEW LIFE?

On the day after Christmas our eldest daughter, fifteen-years-old, squeezed two oranges and carried the glass of orange juice upstairs to the room where her grandmother was sleeping. She knocked, opened the door and discovered that her grandmother was dead. She loved her grandmother, Amah, very much. The world our daughter knew ceased to exist and began anew.

There would be no more long walks for grandmother and granddaughter, no talks by the fire, no stories from favorite books, no recitation and learning of poetry. These would become memories, important memories that the granddaughter treasured. So too, the daily presence of her grandmother,

her influence and patterns of thought would become a continuing part of our daughter's life. Amah was no longer living and breathing, but her influence remained and increased. In new, unknown ways, Amah was present, more and more, as Sarah grew into the woman she was to become. Amah was her model as Sarah became the person she was intended to be.

Everything that begins anew comes into its fullness only after something else has ended. Death and loss and pain give birth to new life. It never fails.

The Pulitzer Prize for Fiction in 2004 was won by Edward P. Jones for his very first novel, *The Known World*. The small statement in the *New York Times* announcing the award noted that Mr. Jones lived in Arlington, Virginia, where he had worked as a proofreader until he lost his job. Then he began to write, authored a collection of short stories, and then his first novel. Edward Jones was willing to open the door, enter a new as yet unrealized world. What did he find? New Life.

There is an ancient and universal human longing that emerges in all cultures, places and times. All human beings long for immortality—the everlasting continuation of everything—on and on—just as we know it right now. This universal desire is believed to be comforting; this is what human beings have long wanted to believe. But were immortality to be possible, would it be life giving or stultifying? Somehow it brings to mind a golf addict facing retirement who says, "Aha! A future full of nothing but golf, month after month after month." The chances are about 100% that if a single person spent six months doing nothing but playing golf, day after day after day, when the six months ended, he'd be ready to do anything else, anything at all.

Fortunately, we are not immortal. Deep down, we all know that there is only one constant in our lives—change. The change that emerges after death is marked by new life.

Romance, the electricity that exists between two people who share a life-long love, should be and can be constantly renewed. But the thrill that comes when we fall in love for the very first time happens only once. The memory of moonlight and the words "I love you" spoken for the first time do not happen again, but if a life of real romance is to continue, then new words, new memories, new miracles emerge.

What results from change is called new life. It turns time and the future and the present upside down, putting it on a new footing. It means that when one thing ends, when one person and one experience and one moment cease to exist, there will be something else, something new. The new will not be the same as the old. It will be very different.

The opportunity for change does not necessarily mean moving to a new environment. Years ago, weeks after becoming headmaster, I hired a young man, just out of college to start a program of community service long before it was known and popular. He did a first rate job, so good that he taught basic courses in the middle school that would lay the foundation for his work in community service. He taught and worked with students in the middle school so well that he then became the Director of the middle school. This responsibility meant he was more and more invested in the real nuts and bolts, the finances of the operation. He became assistant to the Business Manager and then Business Manager. He never did the same job for more than five years. His professional life was marked by change, yet he worked for the same school for forty years.

Change and freshness and new challenge were constantly present.

Everything that begins, ends. Do not expect it to be otherwise. Change is painful, and the pain is life-long. When the wife you have lived with and loved for fifty years dies, there will be no consolation. When you get fired from the job in which you have invested your life, you will be completely and absolutely destroyed. When you get to the top of the ladder you have been climbing for most of your life and find that it is leaning against the wrong wall, it will be too late to start over again. But be not afraid. Change is not all. There is more.

> ℰ She died after a long illness, the loss deeply felt by all who knew her, none more than her children and grandchildren. What happened then was that each member of her family who had been left behind sought and found new direction. Since she who had led and embodied the family was no longer living, the mantle of all that she embodied and made possible now fell on those who were left behind. No one of them was ever the same again.

❦ The dismissal from his job was unexpected, unannounced, swift and cruel. One day he was on the way up, and the next he was out. His career was over. After he picked himself up and assessed the situation, he decided to become an author, consultant, public figure and speaker. Twenty years later, when he and his wife looked back over fifty years of marriage, both agreed that these new years, the last twenty, had been the happiest of their life together.

❦ When the cancer was first diagnosed in his spinal cord, the only effective procedure to attempt a cure was to remove it, surgically. The operation left him paralyzed, consigned to a wheel chair, still not cancer free. Then a new procedure removed all of the cancer. Too late. Now he was cured, healthy but still paralyzed. He continued his successful writing career. The next book he wrote bore the title, *A Whole New Life*. Here he proclaimed eloquently and completely that his new life was not only different but superior to the fifty years he had already lived.

New life is more significant, long-lasting, overpowering than death. You can not see into it; the future is a mystery. You can not control it. You can not predict it. What you can do is to open yourself to allow it to happen. Be prepared. Be responsive. Give thanks.

CHAPTER ONE

Is This All?

NEW LIFE has the power to change, direct and fulfill your professional career. But it all depends on your willingness to ask yourself two essential questions. The first is: "Is this all?"

Forty years ago Betty Friedan's question on the first page of *The Feminine Mystique* changed the world for women and their vocational lives. Today, this is the question every person needs to ask at least once—perhaps several times—in his or her professional career. When you ask that question—listen. Pay attention to what you hear. It's time for change.

"Is this all?" Friedan asked on behalf of young women whose single focus as wives and mothers was becoming diffuse, less than all encompassing, no longer captivating. Few people had ever asked such a question in that or any circumstance, and when it was asked, asked in earnest, the world changed.

When and how should this question be asked?

~

Charles Allen has lived his entire life in Savannah, where he was born and means to remain. Twenty years ago he became editor of *Southern Daily News*. As a boy, Charles had dreamed that some day this would be his job. Now it is.

Charles has worked with two different publishers, each an owner. The first, Byron, was given to temper and drink, unpredictable, except during weekly staff meetings, when Charles was the focus of his discontents. Charles never wavered. The quality of his work steadily improved. Almost ten years ago, George Sampson succeeded Byron. George is an academic: quiet, steady, dramatically able, widely admired. The reputation of the *Southern Daily News* has substantially increased; sales and circulation have constantly improved and are now deemed outstanding in every regard.

Two years ago Charles's life changed when George created the position of executive assistant to the publisher, a person charged with the oversight of all operations. Charles reported to the executive assistant, not an easy adjustment. More difficult still was a new system of performance review, instituted by the new assistant. Charles met regularly with the publisher and his executive assistant to review every aspect of his work. The conversations were difficult, but Charles endured them.

An annual performance review took place. Charles's memory of the conversation is clouded. He remembers entering the publisher's office as George opened the door and greeted him and the executive assistant. Their chairs were triangulated. Something felt wrong. Then Charles heard George speaking.

"Charles," George said, "Charles, the time has come to make a change. We've decided to go in a new direction."

The three men had scarcely seated themselves around the enormous rug in the paneled office. It was hot, very hot.

Charles straightened, as if hit by an electric shock, and exclaimed, "What are you talking about? What are you saying? I've been here twenty years, day and night, most weeks. Twenty years. And you're telling me...?"

"Charles, I'm telling you you've been great, superb." George added. "No one better. Neither the *News* nor this publisher could have asked for more. But the time has come, Charles. We're going to make a change."

Charles stood and began to pace. The executive assistant sat over in the corner, silent, immobile. George started to speak, but Charles burst out, "I don't understand. I just don't understand. I thought you liked me. That's what you've told me again and again. Liked me. Valued my work. Your predecessor was the one who made my life miserable. You and I have worked well together. I've produced. And now you're telling me to leave, that I've been fired." He raised his hands in desperation and crumpled onto the huge leather couch.

"Not a bit. Nothing like that. 'Fired' is not the word, Charles. It's just that there comes a time, you know, you've seen it. Nothing lasts forever. Change is good. Good for you, good for us."

"Good? *Good!* Just what's good about it? What do you have in mind for me to do? *What do you have in mind for me to do?* Savannah and the *News* are my life, my whole life. And now you're telling me to start over."

Charles raced to the door and stormed out. George started to stand, wanting to do something, be in charge, shake Charles's hand, but slumped back into his chair. The executive assistant sat still as stone, looking more like a gargoyle than a person.

Could this have been avoided? Should Charles have seen it coming? No dream job lasts forever, especially one that begins at thirty-eight. George should have seen this. Charles should have seen this. Neither did. Nothing had been done.

Is Charles's situation true for others? Is it true for you? How long is long enough? When is it right to ask, "Is This All?"

~

Bob Edwards of *Morning Edition* and National Public Radio originated *Morning Edition* and presided over it for close to twenty-five years. Edwards and *Morning Edition* were enormously successful. It was Bob Edwards who was completely responsible for inspiring Joan Kroc, of McDonald's fame and fortune, to make a gift of $200 million to NPR. The gift and its size were astounding. Nothing like this had ever happened before. But, once the gift was in hand, and Mrs. Kroc's body was in the ground, NPR announced that Bob Edwards was being moved out from the position he had established and made successful. It was time for a new approach, a faster pace, persons who were more in keeping with the speed and tempo of the world that *Morning Edition* existed to report.

It was abundantly clear this change was not Mr. Edwards's choice. The outrage of listeners far and wide was loud and vocal. Letters and emails and telephone calls arrived by the thousands upon thousands. No matter. Bob Edwards went on tour looking for a new life.

~

Christine has always been a thoughtful person. Active and athletic while growing up, she was reflective, lived "inside her head," read well beyond her grade level, asked questions and listened carefully to answers.

Chris attended Walnut Hills in Cincinnati, a selective magnet high school, and went on to Williams College, where she majored in religion, surrounded by a supportive community of persons, teachers and students, who wrestled with important, sometimes ultimate, questions. She flourished at Williams, became a leader, widely and well respected. After graduation it was a natural transition for Chris to achieve considerable success in international investment and finance, specializing in establishing American businesses in China. She was fulfilled and successful.

At about age fifty, however, the questions that had never left her recurred in new forms. One way or another, she kept hearing herself say, "Is this all?" The goals she had set earlier in life had been achieved. Now she wanted a new challenge that would make it possible to leave a lasting mark on the world around her while engaged in a pursuit she truly valued.

Given the connections and contacts she

had made throughout her lifetime and relying extensively on her relationship to Williams College, Chris found work as a comptroller in a premiere New England boarding school, where she was also able to teach, read and write extensively and explore conclusively the questions with which she had wrestled throughout her adult life.

Chris had asked the question, "Is this all?" and when she heard the answer, "No," she acted thoughtfully and decisively.

~

My uncle's professional career has made a deep imprint on me. When he was fifty years old, he faced a significant vocational crossroad. As a prominent trial and corporate lawyer, his legal expertise, Workmen's Compensation, required almost daily court appearances, frequent arguments before the Massachusetts Supreme Court and untold hours with physicians. This resulted in new, close friends, who were often in our house for meals and conversation. These new friendships produced a fresh, increasingly intense interest in medicine, a fascination that grew so strong that if my uncle had done what he truly wanted to do, he would have gone to medical school and started his professional life all over again.

Hindsight, renowned for being 20/20, tells me that if my uncle, having proved himself in one arena, wanted to redirect his professional life at age fifty, that aim could have been life-giving. As might have been anticipated, however, family, financial and professional considerations intervened. Such a step—completely changing careers at midlife—was clearly impossible, and the response my uncle received on every side was a resounding, "No!"

At almost the very same time, quite by coincidence and out of the blue, my uncle received an offer to join a prominent New York law firm. The new job would have doubled his salary, but life in New York City is more expensive than any other city, sometimes twice as expensive. Besides, my aunt and uncle had never lived in New York; they'd always lived in Boston. The offer was declined.

My uncle chose a third course. Rather than a new beginning in medicine or a move to New

York City, he chose to become the General Counsel for the insurance company he and his law firm had long served. Redirection at mid-life gave way to a safer, more acceptable course: to continue to do essentially the same thing in the same place.

But not indefinitely. My uncle had a plan, a good plan. The President and General Manager of the insurance company for whom my uncle worked was his friend of thirty years. He was a very good friend. The plan was to work closely with the President, and then, succeed him.

That never happened. Those were the days before mandatory retirement. The President worked until he was 77. By that time my uncle was 63. He was passed over, put out to pasture. Accompanied by his long-serving secretary, he was given a new, spacious office in a nearby building, each window commanding a magnificent view of the harbor. The only problem was that he was given nothing to do. He lived for only three more years. "Is This All?" is a life or death question. It is the question that forces you to realize that everything upon which your future depends hangs in the balance.

CHAPTER TWO

What's Next

The second question essential to the process of NEW LIFE is "What's Next?"

When I was forty-two years old, I was happier and more completely fulfilled, professionally and vocationally, than at any time in my life. Headmaster for five years, the school I served was growing and prospering. But I knew enough to know that nothing lasts forever. I sought a professional person who could help me evaluate where I was and where I should go when the time was right.

The person I chose was Charles MacArthur, then Director of the Harvard Grant Study, a longitudinal study of a group of several hundred Harvard graduates from the late 1930s and early 1940s—all anonymous, but one was rumored to have become President of the United States. Participants had been chosen for their promise and the presumed good health of their family. What has been written about this study, especially by the current director, George Valliant, is fascinating.

MacArthur and I met four times: twice for conversation and twice for testing. He was fascinated with my ability for organization.

"Keep doing what you are doing." He'd say. "You're perfect at it. Just do it someplace else."

"Where?" I'd ask.

"Well, why not become President of Harvard?" He really said that.

MacArthur made me feel good about what I was doing, but he was dumbfounded by my question: "What next?" He was caught unaware. Had he never heard anyone ask that question? Everyone should. But how? How do people come to realize that they must ask this question, for themselves? When it comes up in some other way, as surely it will, sooner or later, it can be a recipe for disaster.

There are persons and agencies that attempt to answer this question from their own perspectives that are sometimes quite different from yours and not necessarily helpful.

The crucial turning point on which NEW LIFE hinges is not your central interest, not your transferable skills and how your next position will employ those skills. Rather, the crucial and determining factor of NEW LIFE is one of motivation: the courage, the drive, the willingness to ask the question, "What's next?"

Where do you find the motivation to ask that question and to take the risk? How do you overcome such roadblocks as these?

- ℰ Location: am I willing to move?

- ℰ Spouse: will he or she allow me to change jobs?

- ℰ Pension: is it portable?

- ℰ Health insurance: who will cover me and my family?

- ℰ Children's schools: will they be willing to leave them?

When we moved back to Washington, D.C. in 1987 to undertake new lives at age 53, we were told to look up Fisher Howe. Fisher graduated from Harvard College in 1935, which means he has now passed his 90th birthday. I first met him for lunch at The Metropolitan Club when he was only seventy-five. His office was six blocks away on Rhode Island Avenue. "How did you get here?" I inquired. "I ran. I exercise for an hour and try to eat six different fruits or vegetables every day."

After college, Fisher entered the Foreign Service, had a full and active career, retired years ago, and then entered his second graduate program at Johns Hopkins, only to be called back to the Foreign Service to be involved in arms negotiations. When this second career in the Foreign Service ended, Fisher joined the staff of Johns Hopkins to work in development, and this led him to become a member of a consulting firm that helped direct fundraising campaigns. In time Fisher became the principal and owner of the firm. Fisher's initial and primary professional career ended more than thirty years ago. Since then he has had three, four, five different careers, depending on how you count them.

Fisher agrees that new life is essential but believes it has to be entirely self-motivated. It is impossible to create it for another person. Nothing except the loss of a job and the desperate need to find a new job will motivate it. It is my conviction that new life is motivated by asking and answering the question: "What's next?"

The absolute necessity for new career direction at mid-life is going to happen to vast numbers of people. Experience has taught me how best to direct this change and help to make it happen.

My grandfather created his own professional experience in a way that has also made a great impression on me. He may not have had the luxury to ask the question, "What's next?" but he surely answered the question.

Born in 1861 on a farm near Moncton, New Brunswick, one of nine children, Bapapa (whose real name was Job) attended a local business college, then moved to Boston, met and married my grandmother. He was bright and handsome, personable, engaging. He started a small real estate and insurance business and was unusually successful for a young man who began with nothing. He prospered, moved to better and better neighborhoods, sent his only daughter to Girls' Latin, the best girls' high school in the country, and then to Smith College. When she married, he built her a new house, right nearby, up over the hill. Bapapa knew a thing or two about control.

Then came the Depression. Bapapa was in his late fifties. He lost everything. His business was gone. He was wiped out. He started all over, created a new business, purchased small, unusual properties, one at a time. Each property was located in or near Park Square, which he maintained was the direction of the future. It was where the new City of Boston finally did move. When Job Gaskin died, the man I called Bapapa, he was not a wealthy man, but he did leave behind much property and a great deal for me to think about when I stop to look at the photographs of him that cover my study walls.

At the time of his death, my grandfather had worked more than thirty-five years *after* becoming bankrupt and losing everything. He never retired, never wanted to retire. He went to a favorite vacation hotel in Florida in the winter months where, day after day, he played bridge with countless lady friends and then went to another such hotel in Maine for some weeks each summer. Otherwise, he was in his office at 224 Stuart Street virtually every working day.

Perhaps I should have asked him if the outcome of his life had been shaped by his bankruptcy and the absolute necessity to start all over again. After all, it happened well after mid-life and at a time when most persons are getting ready to stop work. Motivation was never an option or a question. Or was it? Some driving force entered his life and changed it.

It was the question, "What's next?"

CHAPTER THREE

The Master Word is Work

Sir William Osler, the great Canadian physician (1849-1919) is known for his philosophy of work, first articulated in public before an assembly of medical students at the inauguration of new laboratories at Toronto and Trinity Universities in 1903:

Though a little one, the master word looms large in meaning. It is the open sesame to every portal, the great equalizer in the world, the true philosopher's stone which transmutes the base metal of humanity into gold. The stupid man among you it will make bright, the bright man brilliant, and the brilliant steady. With the master word in your heart all things are possible, and without it all study is vanity and vexation. The miracles of life are with it; the blind see by touch, the deaf hear with eyes, the dumb speak with fingers. To the youth it brings hope, to the middle-aged confidence, to the aged repose. True balm of hurt minds, in its presence the heart of the sorrowful is lightened and consoled... And the master word is work, *a little one, but fraught with momentous consequences if you can but write it on the tables of your heart and bind it upon your forehead.*

Work as the centerpiece, the very reason for being, was emphasized, again and again, when I was a child. It became a way of life, anything but a burden. Osler's words were read, repeated, recommended, exhorted. Work, I learned, is the extension of the self; work is the self, blown large and present in the world with and for others.

My father believed in the work ethic for which New Englanders once were famous. Before the summer I was to turn sixteen, he announced that the time had come for me to go to work—full time. The summer job chosen was as postal clerk on the mail boat that delivered mail, six days a week, ten weeks of the summer, to one hundred families, who lived on the shores of Squam Lake in New

Hampshire, where our family spent the summer. It was an ideal job, but it was six days a week and lasted all summer long.

There was one problem. The person who held this job had to be sixteen years of age. My sixteenth birthday was still weeks away. But my father knew John McCormick, Speaker of the United States House of Representatives, who got in touch with the Postmaster General, who called the small rural post office in New Hampshire.

Said the postmaster to his wife: "Well, Genevieve, if we have to hire someone else and pay for him ourselves to do the work, that's what we'll have to do. This Gleason boy is going to be clerk. No two ways about it."

I went to work. There were sacrifices. I never learned to play tennis or golf as well as I might; my promising skill as a fisherman fell into disuse, and disappeared. Something else took its place: the celebration and appreciation of work.

Work *was* a way of life, and work meant pursuing a profession. A profession is defined as more than what one does to earn a living; a profession is how one makes a life. It means professing what matters most. Originally, the professions included only medicine, law, teaching, the ministry. They now embrace other worthy pursuits.

My own orientation to work and vocation that began with Osler was further expanded by two other formative experiences.

During the third and fourth grades I attended the local elementary school. Gas rationing meant that I walked each morning down the hill, one mile, to school, back at mid-day, down again in the afternoon, home at four. As I walked, I was all alone, living in my imagination, exploring unknown worlds. I vowed I would never lose the ability to create and enter these worlds through my imagination. Maturity is marked by the ability to project one's self into the future and evaluate different possibilities. If one can understand the prospects of the future, then one can live into them.

When the time came to wrestle with the idea of vocation, I understood this process differently from others. Work—how to spend most waking hours as a grown, professional person—was a commitment to a way of life, constructed through imagination that projected me into different futures.

This was further enhanced by another experience. My family introduced me to older men, whose professions interested me, for whom work was more than a way to earn a living. These friends of my parents were often in our house, at our table, part of our summer community. All were professionals, many academics and clergy, sometimes both. These were my adult models, the people I wanted to become.

Vocation is one of the primary choices each person makes. Another is the choice of mate. Each choice involves a way of life; taken together, the two fashion the great end and real business of living. Each choice should remain a living, growing entity, frequently reaffirmed, deepened.

Years ago the central point of the Broadway comedy, "The Seven Year Itch" was really not amusing. It made a joke out of the wanderlust that arises in a marriage approximately every seven years. This reality is an opportunity for reaffirmation, and if it does not happen, the marriage ends. I remember a conversation with a dear friend who lamented the end of the marriage of another couple after thirty-two years. "What a waste," he said. "What a waste. All those years married to the wrong person."

"Not at all," I replied. "It was an excellent marriage. The two of them just failed to move ahead to a new level of commitment. Vows need to be reaffirmed."

True of marriage. True of vocation. One's commitment is constantly to be understood in new and deeper ways. The calling in life that one chooses to profess must constantly evolve. There is an initial flush of excitement and attraction that draws you that can not be maintained; it is too immediate. The passion that excites you continues in different forms. The same profession but different expressions.

~

Frances grew up in a family founded on the belief that all things were possible. The eldest of three, from her earliest years Frances understood that challenges existed to be met and overcome; she thrived on them. An early and voracious reader, lovely to look upon, she established herself as an academic leader.

Often the best student in her class, Frances's love of the physical and athletic meant that she also became outstanding at team and individual sports. As she grew older, Frances undertook responsibility for the cooking in her family. She wanted her career-oriented parents to devote "family" time to conversation with their three daughters. Evening meals, eaten around the dining room table, were the central event of the day. Conversation mattered. Each member cared, each member contributed, each member learned.

When grandmother visited, they listened to stories from long ago. Mother and father reminisced about their childhood friendships, lessons remembered, stories told, facts that mattered. Frances and her sisters rehearsed the day's events, conversations, activities, insights. There were no secrets; dinner table conversation belonged only to those around the table, no one else. Nothing was to be repeated outside the family.

Frances so enjoyed everything about her life that it was difficult to say what mattered most. Life was of one fabric, each part a piece of the whole. One thing led naturally, inevitably, to another, and then, almost seamlessly, she was in college, majoring in English, reading, re-reading, writing, re-writing. She determined writing mattered most; it was evident to Frances that if she wrote clearly and well, then she could do almost anything she wished. It was her understanding that the ability to write was the essential building block to every undertaking.

When Frances graduated from college, she had no idea what to do with the rest of her life. Without a great deal of thought—it just seemed to make sense—she followed the path of least resistance and went to graduate school. Law school was the easiest, all-purpose choice. She had no intention of joining a big New York firm or becoming a trial lawyer. She believed law was a basic building block, a tool she could use.

Nothing about law school was enjoyable, except for the people she met. The first year was agony. Classes were humiliating, the work endless, all of it apparently routine, but she survived and actually did very well.

When graduation drew near, she sought interviews with large corporations, who appeared day after day to recruit. After much thought, Frances finally accepted an attractive offer from Procter and Gamble and moved to Cincinnati, where a number of friends from college and graduate school now lived. Bill, presently employed by a large Cincinnati law firm, was the closest of these friends, and she was thrilled to be able to see him again, and he to see her.

The work with P&G was challenging, if not always interesting, but more and more Frances was frustrated by the top-down structure. Her ideas rose up, hit a ceiling and disappeared. The promise for advancement and the compensation were fine, but Frances felt inhibited, unable to express her own natural talent, especially the ability to write and think clearly. She wanted out.

The "out" she chose was to establish her own small marketing firm. At first she had only one client, but she was lucky to have that one. Then there were more. Her creativity blossomed; the firm prospered. By now she and Bill were married, and his law practice was on track. It was a good life. When Henrietta, their first child, was born, Frances's business was well established. It was stable enough to run on its own for six months before Frances was willing to commit Henrietta's care to a woman in the neighborhood.

As each client and its product line led to another and yet another, there was more work to do than Frances could handle. Her interests broadened more and more, especially when Robert was born and Henrietta entered kindergarten. The business was Frances's creation, but it was healthy enough to be run by another. Frances made her first associate, Cynthia, who had joined her when the company was only months old, Executive Director, put herself on salary as a consultant and went to work full-time as the Assistant Director of the Food Bank, Cincinnati's answer to feeding the poor and homeless.

~

Frances is a single example that could be repeated countless times. In the beginning she chose one path, among many, to fulfill herself as a working person. Then she discovered that the path she chose was not at all limiting. Quite the opposite. It could open, not once, but several times, into new and different directions. The life of work contains continuing, changing and evolving, possibilities. If this is to be true, however, one has to be open and responsive to these possibilities, if they are going to happen. Frances has now reached mid-life. She has come to this point having explored and found herself professionally in a series of quite different situations. She faces a bright future knowing that she has the experience and the ability to continue to re-create herself. Since this is her expectation, her life will continue evolving as it should.

~

Christopher grew up in a family where language held the highest currency. At home and around the dinner table parents and grandparents spoke Italian, as did Christopher, an only child. Italian was the primary language, but English the language of choice. All family members were at the very least bilingual.

Latin was the language of the liturgy on Sundays, holy days and many others, when family and friends gathered for Mass. Language was more than a medium of communication for Christopher; it was the embodiment, the center, of life's meaning. Words led to insight, awareness and finally deeper wisdom. This understanding, so present in his immediate family, set Christopher apart from others. He expected more, grasped more, was more ready to seek connections, knew instinctively there was an added dimension.

On his seventh birthday Christopher and his friend, Thomas, were taken fishing out in the harbor by Christopher's father. The day was bright and sunny, a soft breeze, ideal summer weather. As they passed the outer bell buoy, father set out a line for each boy, and they began to fish for stripers.

Christopher had the first strike, a sizable fish, played long and well. After he brought the fish closer and closer to the boat, Christopher did an unusual thing. He passed his rod to Thomas and grabbed his friend's rod for his own. Thomas played the fish out and brought it alongside for father to gaff. Right then, Christopher had a second, bigger, strike.

These were the only fish of the day. They had been laid together, side by side, silent and huge in the open cooler, staring up out of their dead eyes as the boat headed for home. Father turned in the cockpit. "A good day, boys. A memorable day. And what did you two learn?"

Thomas was the first to speak. "I'll never

have a better friend. Chris is the best."

"He's a great kid. No doubt about it," father added, "What do you say, Christopher?"

The silence was noticeable. "When something good happens to you, share it." He paused: "There's always more."

The story of Christopher's seventh birthday was told often, became the parable of Christopher's life. He lived it and often asked others, "What's yours? What's the moment in your life that changed everything?"

Christopher's parable meant that as his life unfolded, each moment led on to the next, he knew he was a person who was always becoming. There was always more.

Lacrosse was a serious part of Christopher's college life, but his real interest was philosophy and religion. He valued questions, not for the answers, but the questions themselves. One question above all others consumed him. If timing is everything, how do I determine the best time? He remembered his father telling him, "The time to trim the holly bush is when the shears are sharp." Was this an all-purpose answer and everything else elaboration? Whatever the challenge, the time to act was now. It was true that there was no time like the present, even though "in the present" doesn't really exist. Christopher thought of the present as nothing more than the instant, so brief that it was really non-existent, the intersection of the past and the future.

After college Christopher worked for three years with his father learning the rudiments of real estate and insurance business in Athol, Massachusetts. Although father and son enjoyed each other and worked well together, each knew this was not the final answer for Christopher's vocational life. At his father's urging and following his own interest, Christopher was led naturally to business school.

He liked everything about it and made fast and good friends, especially among the other members of his study group. They were such good friends and so like-minded that they knew, almost from the beginning, that they would work together, and they did.

After graduation they formed a venture capital group, *Present Opportunity, Inc.,* working in two areas of specialty in Omaha, Nebraska, where no such group had ever existed. The point of the story is not that *Present Opportunity* was extremely successful, which was never really a question, given the talent of its owners, the economic climate, their location and their specialty, the point is what happened next.

Christopher was not yet fifty years old, married with two children, one in grade school, the other in middle school, and he had more money than he would ever need. Flying his own plane to fish or play golf at different elite spots throughout the world, or even six weeks in Europe each spring for the French Open and Wimbledon didn't make a life, not for a man of Christopher's interests and convictions. He was already a member of the Board of his independent school and college, where worthy and important contribution mattered, but this too was not a life's work. Other worthy non-profits beckoned—look alikes, smaller scale efforts that followed in the train of organizations like City Year, Save the Children and the World Peace Federation. Christopher believed in all these, passionately, philosophically, even religiously, but none was work, none offered a fabric into which and around which Christopher could weave himself. Despite all that he had been able to create and accomplish, there was more. That more was what he sought.

The study group in business school had existed in one time and place, but those associations, those ties, those friendships and connections still existed. These were the resource to which Christopher turned to create his new life.

~

Those are but two stories of many—thousands —that could and should be told. Others will be found throughout this book. The point of each one, and all of them taken together, is that you, the reader, are in the midst of creating your own.

My father once wrote, "... you can not buy with gold the old associations." But those 'old associations' can open the door to NEW LIFE.

CHAPTER FOUR

There's Always More

The more that is to come in your life will emerge from what has gone before. The new appears through the persons and places and networks that know you and know what you know and can do. Your new life will grow from your academic training, life and work experience, your own hard work and what you have done through interaction with others.

When you face the question, "What's next?" it is essential to understand how it is that you arrived where you are. You need to be thoroughly aware of each step on the way, how it was accomplished, how one step followed another and why. The process is completely logical and orderly. Your knowledge of it will lead you into your future. Your process needs to be clearly known and understood. Here is mine. It is but one example.

~

When I was five years old, I wanted to be a doctor. Office hours, physical examinations of my Teddy Bear and medical consultations were part of each day. At the age of ten I wrote a research paper on the types and causes of cancer. It included hand-painted illustrations of cancer cells all contained in a small brown notebook.

My medical interest ceased very abruptly when I was twelve. My father allowed me to convince him to arrange for us to witness an operation at the Massachusetts General Hospital. The two of us, accompanied by a doctor friend and neighbor stood on an observation deck looking down through a glass ceiling into the operating theatre below. The operation was an emergency appendectomy. I can still see the patient surrounded by the medical team, the incision and then an enormous stream of white pus that erupted like a geyser, drained from the wound into a basin. Shortly before I fainted, I had turned away and walked into the corridor, leaving behind any desire to pursue medicine.

At age fifty, when I was still young, my father was converted to Christianity, baptized, confirmed, and became deeply involved in the life of Christian faith, our parish and the Episcopal Church. Now the most interesting and frequent visitors in our house and around our table were prominent and notable clergy. I can still see those men and hear their conversation. Most vivid was the moment after a summer Sunday service when a Park Avenue cleric, whom I held in great awe, put his hand on my arm, looked me straight in the eye, and said to me, "Teddy. You should go to seminary."

The dinner table was the center of our family life. This was *the* place of learning. When conversation turned to my vocational future, my father limited the choice to the professions, strictly and classically understood—law, medicine, teaching, the ministry, and perhaps business. Many influences directed me towards the ordained ministry.

~

During my final year at seminary I was a member of a twelve student seminar. The instructor, Phil Smith, former Rector of Christ Church, Exeter, New Hampshire, new to the faculty of the seminary, came to know me well. Asked by his successor, to recommend a candidate for the position of curate in Exeter, a specific job with particular demands, funded and created while Phil was rector, he recommended me. An interview followed, but the decision had really already taken place. The interview was to determine the comfort level, the challenge, the opportunity—what was the tone and quality of each for the two persons involved who knew me and knew what I knew and could do.

This was the first position of my professional life. The necessary principles that made it unfold were determined by simple rules: who knew me and who knew what I knew and could do.

~

No job lasts forever. The position of curate in Christ Church, Exeter was pre-established to last two years. The end of the two years approached. Leads developed, nothing was in place. Then a telephone call, out of the blue.

A voice said, "Ted, this is Holt Graham."

Holt was an extraordinarily important teacher of mine, who taught the introductory course in New Testament, New Testament Greek, and a course in Paul's Letter to the Romans. He was a distant, quiet, interior man, whose teaching was brilliant; my grades from him were all A's.

On the very first day of class in New Testament he told us that each of us would write a paper on our understanding of the life and ministry of Jesus. We would do it in whatever way was best for each of us. It could range in length from six to eighty pages. There would be no grade. No one understood the enormity of the assignment. If properly approached and undertaken the task would take a hundred hours.

When my paper was returned, I could not wait to read: "This paper is theologically dead center." Holt Graham was my teacher, but he and I communicated on a crucial level.

Soon after my graduation, Holt had been hired, part-time, for two years, as Minister in

Charge of a new congregation—two hundred adults and children who had started a new parish, on their own, to escape the dictatorial, alcoholic ways of the rector of their former parish. This group of competent and well-educated people worshiped in an elementary school. Holt Graham provided clerical leadership on Sundays. Two years passed and then the time came to replace Holt with a full-time Rector.

The search committee turned to Holt for professional insight and advice. Several candidates interviewed; I was Holt's choice. The search committee did its work, but the matter was decided through Holt Graham, an important person from my past, a person who knew me and knew what I knew. The process took place virtually in spite of me, outside my knowledge and sphere of influence.

~

Professionally and vocationally, this new job was an extraordinary opportunity for someone of my age and situation. Two years out of seminary, twenty-eight years old, I was responsible for a self-sustaining and wealthy congregation in a rapidly growing suburban neighborhood in greater Washington, D. C. Six acres of land had been purchased, plans for a building drawn, the congregation growing. A year and a half later we were in our own building, and I hired a full-time clergy assistant. Surely I would remain for a long time.

Christ Church, Exeter made ready to dedicate a new building. I was asked to preach. The service was an extravaganza, and the participants included the new Principal of The Phillips Exeter Academy, Richard Ward Day, whom I met there for the very first time. That meeting resulted months later in a new job as School Minister. The pieces that made it all happen did not fit together immediately, but they were present that evening. Such pieces are present and active in your life—right now—but you need to set into action a series of actions that will discern them, fit them together, act to help them mobilize and change your life. It is that simple, but it is not something you do alone.

~

The four years I was employed as School Minister in The Phillips Exeter Academy were as demanding and fulfilling as any of my life. The years 1967 to 1971 were a time of social and political turmoil and change that had a profound effect upon a large, well-established boarding school created to serve intellectually able boys from every quarter. While my relationships with colleagues and students were formative, Dick Day, was pivotal, the mentor of my mid-thirties.

Dick Day knew who he was; he had a clear sense of his own identity. He also knew he wanted to move his institution forward and would do so by hiring good people, giving them responsibility, encouraging and supporting them. He had vision; he was demanding, and he was always right there—beside and behind me.

What he wanted was challenging, but once he knew who you were and what you could and would do, then he opened doors and created opportunities. I learned from him and I learned with him, but what I never completely realized was that he was preparing me to become a headmaster. Once I had done the job he expected, then he began to circulate my name, but he did not support a positive decision until the choice I made coincided with his.

The chairman of the Exeter Board of Trustees was a close friend and law partner of the chairman of the search committee of Noble and Greenough School. Day recommended me with great enthusiasm. Even as the first interview began, and before it had ended, I knew that this was it—and so did the search committee. What I did not realize was the positive energy that had preceded me, thanks to Day's recommendation, the respect in which he was held and that he held for me. The job was virtually assured from the outset. It had all depended on who knew me and who knew what I knew and could do.

~

There had been a time when one ran a school for a professional lifetime. No longer. Ten years came and went. Life was challenging, the school growing and changing, and although I was happily occupied, I began to cast tentatively in other directions. Nothing came together; there was no one who knew me, knew what I knew and could do.

Increasingly restless, after much thought I accepted a sabbatical that had been available for some time, knowing I would not return, for I was ready to get away from that particular daily round and wanted to write a book much more than I wanted to run a school. We set off across the country to live in Santa Fe and follow our dream.

We had not been in residence for ten days, when after a morning of writing, sitting on the front porch eating lunch, the telephone rang. It was the Dean of Virginia Theological Seminary. "Ted," he said, "You wouldn't want to be the Director of Development for the Seminary, would you?"

The offer may have been stated negatively, but when Dick Reid spoke the words, I knew that I would accept. First there was a process. We thought a great deal about the future, talked and planned. Were there other possibilities? Before it all came to a conclusion, this happened.

Unable to write longer that particular morning, I'd wandered downtown. There was an errand, but mostly, I wanted time to think.

An important decision loomed. What was next?

The walk nearly over, I was headed up Maury Street towards Hillcrest Avenue, where we lived, when a pickup truck, bearing the sign, PIGEON DELIVERY SERVICE, INC., came down the hill towards me, wheeled into the curb on the passenger's side.

"Excuse me for minding somebody else's business," the driver said, "But you look like a fellow with something on his mind."

"As a matter of fact," I replied, "I'm trying to decide what to do with the rest of my life, or at least the next few years."

By this time I'd opened the door and climbed into the passenger's seat. Richard Bradshaw Odell IV and I had shaken hands and said good morning. We did not know one another well, but we had met, more than once, at the 7:00 a.m. Eucharist at The Church of the Holy Faith. Dick Odell (and four generations of his family) had lived all his life in New Mexico, except the years Dick had spent in Vietnam. One felt comfortable when with Dick Odell. It felt like he owned this place, new to us and all so familiar to him.

"Well," he continued," what are the possibilities?" I told him there were three options. "And do you favor one of them?" I said that I thought no doubt I'd go to Virginia Seminary to be the Director of Development.

"Then do it. Do it. But remember, a job is only a platform, and all platforms are made of wood. Sooner or later they rot. You were born into this world for only one reason: to serve God."

There was a long pause. What else is there to say after a pronouncement like that? It was Dick who broke the silence, "You know, I'd best be on my way, 'cause if I don't get this stuff to Albuquerque by noon, I'll lose the contract." It was time for me to get out. I did.

But as he drove away, he shouted out through the window, "Excuse me for minding your business. You were born into this world for one reason: to serve God."

His unexpected but welcome intervention that Tuesday morning made a big impact. My decision was made. It came about when not just one, but two persons spent some time and effort minding my business—Dick Reid and Dick Odell. I accepted the position as

Director of Development, and we spent eight very fulfilled years in Alexandria. Some one knew me and knew what I knew and what I could do.

~

After twenty years in the world of independent education at a significant distance from the Episcopal Church, I had returned to the church to work as a member of the faculty, Director of Development, Alumni and Alumnae, and Publications in the Virginia Theological Seminary. Once a major capital campaign had been completed and a new program for annual giving and reunions put in place, I was afforded a six-month sabbatical. Just as it began, a member of the Board of Forward Movement Publications called to ask if I would consider the possibility of the position of Editor and Director. Several trips to Cincinnati ensued, a job was offered and accepted, the move to take place at the end of the academic year.

How did that happen? The process to find a replacement for my predecessor was set up and put in motion a full year in advance and followed acceptable practice. Efficient and thorough, after a full year, it had produced no candidate. The committee sat down, faced one another, and it was said, "We did everything we were told to do, and there was no result. Now, let's do it the old fashioned way: whom do you know?"

But the process that led to the telephone call that summoned me was a mystery. It took place in a world beyond my knowledge and outside my control. The result, however, was the same. When the call came and the interview followed, the end result was virtually assumed. What was going to happen was a foregone conclusion.

There is a moral. All of this can easily happen to you.

CHAPTER FIVE

Eyes to See, Ears to Hear, a Heart to Understand

Near the end of my sixteen years as headmaster, I attended a conference directed by David Mallery, a man of indefatigable energy and enthusiasm, who constantly reinvents himself. After the participants had been gathered and introduced themselves, David's first exercise was to place us in groups of four, seated on the grass on the lawn of the conference center. We were asked to outline to our three partners our most immediate challenge; the others were to respond by offering helpful suggestions for a solution.

After we sat, I offered to speak first, saying my challenge was unique and not relevant to others: I was about to leave my position and undertake a totally new life. One of those seated on the grass had just completed his first year as head of school, the second his sixth, the third her fourth. Each immediately volunteered that what to do after their present job was their most pressing and crucial, concern. I was flabbergasted, then realized I was with very able, intelligent, gifted professional persons. Each undertook the same very demanding job with skill and insight; each knew the job was not forever and needed, constantly, to be thinking and planning for the future.

Seventeen years later, one still serves as head of the same independent school, one directs a community foundation in a distant, major American city, and the third serves as a consultant for non-profit organizations.

As I had approached my own moment of change and wrestled with what to do next, I wrote a short article for a professional journal, "After Headmastering... What?" It seemed a difficult and critical question that we prefer not to answer. We must.

NEW LIFE proposes a new approach to help you get to your objective, which is: a new career direction at mid-life and beyond. It is this:

Whatever your education and training, your field of professional expertise, your background, your interests and your transferable skills, your new position will be offered to you through the fortuitous intersection of a group of persons and connections who know you and know what you know and can do.

NEW LIFE is based on the premise that the fortuitous need not be accidental. What often seems to happen as if by chance may happen by choice.

There is an old saying: *The person does not seek the position. The position seeks the person.* The words contain both truth and wisdom. The process by which persons move from job to job operates quite beyond their control. It happens because others, who know him, know what he knows, join together and act on his behalf to bring new opportunities into being.

This process takes place through the natural course of events. NEW LIFE proposes that what once happened independent of the job-seeker can be aided and abetted by an agent working on behalf of the person who seeks NEW LIFE.

Let us examine an actual case history and then ask how might this result—a new career opportunity—have been made to happen.

~

George Fuller has devoted his entire life to independent schools.

When the time came for George to attend kindergarten, his father and mother enrolled him in the nearby, highly esteemed, elementary school, where he spent nine happy years, walking, all by himself, to and from school each day. They were wonderful days as were his days at home. George's was an idyllic childhood: youngest child and only son of a banker father, who also walked to work, and a homemaker mother, who not only cared for her children and husband, but was a leader in the cultural life of the community.

The community placed high value on education. George flourished in school as a student, a leader and an athlete. When his school ended at eighth grade, he entered a boarding school, where he excelled, and he and his two roommates became friends for life. Two attended the same college. George majored in religion, his roommate in design, knowing that he would spend his life designing and building. George thought seriously about seminary, but since his father was less than enthusiastic, he decided that he would consult with the headmaster of his secondary school. He had questions about working in schools, tentative questions; everything was tentative as he prepared to graduate from college.

The headmaster was helpful, full of suggestions of people to see, questions to consider, books to read. They kept talking until the headmaster asked George to become an intern; he needed an eager young man who knew his way around. No money would change hands, but George would have room and board and good experience. George accepted.

George worked in college placement until he was offered an entry level position at a lesser known college. He took it, stayed long enough to find a teaching position in a small

New England boarding school where he met Susie Hardwick. Their years working together as teachers were happy, happy enough to lead to marriage and the move to a new environment.

Newly located, Susie found a job in the very school where George had once been a student, and George a fine position as college placement director, teacher and coach in a nearby independent urban day school.

George and Susie remained in their respective positions for seven years, and then it all came together. They were ready to have a baby, George wanted to run a school, and each of them was ready for a change. A well respected independent school, Southport Academy, in a far away city was looking for new leadership, George's name came to them through several sources, chiefly the headmasters for whom he had worked.

Through thirteen years George took Southport, a good school, and made it far better. The faculty and curriculum were overhauled, a massive fund drive re-built the fabric of the place. George worked extremely hard and well. When it was clear that thirteen years was long enough, a search committee came calling from a larger and more prestigious school in a larger city. The challenges were even greater; George had demonstrated his resourcefulness and capability and took the job and did it extremely well, until he retired twenty years later at the age of seventy-two.

~

That's the way it happened, the way it would appear, the way that the world would have seen and understood it. The question that remains is what would have happened had NEW LIFE become part of George's life as he completed his first thirteen years as headmaster? Could the next phase of his life have taken a quite new and different direction? If so, how might this have taken place? That scenario could look like this.

~

After George had completed ten years at Southport Academy, he was forty-eight years old and had accomplished most of what he had set forth to do. The challenges came daily; nothing was easy, but everything went well. George and his work at Southport were successful. He had made it.

There was no reason to look around or even to think about the future. His predecessor, and the headmaster before his predecessor, who was still serving at Southport before George was born, had stayed in this same job until retirement and then settled in the neighborhood. George could do the same.

It was then that George heard a still small voice saying, over and over again, "If it ain't broke, don't fix it." And George said to himself, "That's just the time to fix it. It's when everything seems perfect that the time has come to see a new approach."

If this was all there was to his life, should he not begin to think about what was next? On the other hand, why bother? Something still ate at him. Should he just sit back and ride it out? Was Southport going to be it? He liked it, he really did. Why, after all, it was he who had created all the spaces that surrounded him. Much as he honestly did not want to give it all up, let it go, something told him that there had to be something more. He was curious to discover what that might be.

But how? The answer: NEW LIFE. He checked the web site, made a telephone call, had a long conversation, received descriptive materials, wrote, as he was requested, a good deal about his past life, present situation and future hopes.

When all this was in hand and evaluated by NEW LIFE, the following took place. Five persons from five different parts of George's life were identified, five persons who knew him well and knew what he knew and what he could do. The five were: 1) the Chairman of the Board of Southport; 2) the Headmaster of the school where George served for seven years; 3) the headmaster of the boarding school where he and Susie worked together; 4) the headmaster of his own secondary school where he had started as an intern; 5) his college roommate who was now a very successful residential developer.

After extensive review, individual conversation and the reading of introductory material, it was arranged for these five to meet through a conference call that might last as long as three hours. Each knew he was being asked to make a major contribution to the life and future of George Fuller, a contribution rooted in their long association and friendship and their personal and professional knowledge.

These were five persons who knew George very well, knew a great deal about what George knew, what he could do and what he had done. What needed to happen was for the five of them to be in one place and at one time—in person or on the telephone—for a significant period of time and to focus on George Fuller. What did each of them know about him? Each of them knew him well but in quite different ways. What did he do best? What were his fondest hopes?

His life had been invested in schools, invested with great advantage to him and for those pupils, parents, trustees and graduates whom he had served. There was no doubt that he could run a school, and do that very well. He'd done so once, and he could do it again. But were there other career possibilities that George might pursue? And once those possibilities had been identified, who were the persons who might open the doors for George to undertake those possibilities?

Here is what happened. As NEW LIFE acted as the moderator and director of this conversation, each man briefly rehearsed some details of his friendship and association with George. There were many stories, good stories of days now passed, and there were often points of intersection and overlap. The picture of George, close to fifty years old and at the peak of his possibility and accomplishment, emerged.

Then, this happened. The Chairman of the Southport Board said, "Our symphony orchestra is looking for a new General Manager. Does anyone think that's the kind of thing George would be interested in doing? He'd sure be good at it."

Now that they thought of it, which no one had before, especially George, all agreed George really would be perfect for such a job. Then someone brought up the fact that when the New York Public Library was looking for a new librarian, they also sought an academic administrator. Did any one know of public library systems that had such a need? As a matter of fact one man knew of just such a need. But then one of the headmasters said that he had a trustee in his city who was putting together a new mutual fund. A person with George's background and interests would be a great addition as a director—not a full-time job, but an interesting entrée. One thing could lead to another.

It was then that his former roommate remembered that there was an investor in the same city where the new mutual fund was being established who was looking for a person to manage his new business.

Each thought, each conversation built upon one, and sometimes more than one, that had preceded it. The level of intensity and involvement built, and the productivity, the usefulness and the vitality of the several different and complimentary contributions increased. The time came, however, when all that could be said on this occasion had been said. NEW LIFE suggested a wrap-up, final comments from each participant, and then said that the convenor would review the tape of the conversation, prepare an executive summary, circulate it to each participant, and then follow up with an individual telephone conversation.

What was the next step? A second conversation that would build on the first but with George present and participating. Could this be arranged, even face-to-face? All agreed that surely there could be another conference call, and perhaps there would be a way to meet all at one time and in one place.

The executive summary and individual conversations having occurred, the group agreed to meet together for a half day at Southport Academy. Three very clear possibilities and the necessary steps to make each of them occur were the final result. These were only the most immediate and realizable. There were others; three stood out:

1) Director of Development for a large city hospital.

2) Manager of a chain of local hardware stores.

3) Librarian for a city-wide system.

None of these possibilities had ever occurred to George Fuller or to anyone else. NEW LIFE brought them to light.

~

George's exploration of NEW LIFE was demanding and involved hundreds of hours of work on the part of several people. It was labor and time intensive, thinking in new ways about old situations. There was nothing easy about the process, but the stakes were high: the best use of the rest of George's life.

The process, however, is often blocked by impediments. It is to these that we must now turn.

CHAPTER SIX

Impediments to NEW LIFE

Fisher Howe has moved seamlessly through several careers during his long and successful professional life. He maintains that the lack of motivation to seek a new career will always stand in the way of NEW LIFE. The person who most needs a new career direction will not want it.

Persons who desperately need to change will not see the need for NEW LIFE. When and if pushed, they may actually refuse to be involved. The only way to include these people in such a program, Fisher contends, will be to force them. Again and again, those who will most benefit from and desperately need a new career direction will be reluctant. What then? If the person who needs to change has no desire, none, to do so, prefers not to move in a new direction, can anything, anything at all, be done?

The thoughtful employer, the person who wants the most for those committed to his care, the boss whose goals for his organization are something more than efficiency and profitability, faces this dilemma, again and again. What to do? Counsel, cajole, offer, encourage? And if all of these fail? Give up? Or should the person be fired?

Unless one believes that there are people in the world who are so totally incompetent that there is literally no new and different job of which they are capable, there are always other—new and different—employment opportunities available. But how does one bring the person who needs such an opportunity to this understanding?

There was a time, and not that long ago, when it was thought that the only way an alcoholic would ever reach the desire to stop drinking was to "hit bottom." A person "hit bottom" by being allowed to drink himself into oblivion, again and again and again, until everything was lost: health, job, marriage, family, house. Then, and only then, it was maintained, will the alcoholic come to his senses and know that he has no power of himself to help himself. Then, and only then, finally, he will turn to a Higher Power, to fellow alcoholics, to the discipline of Alcoholics Anonymous (AA), find sobriety and a new life.

The cost, of course, was enormous. What was left was usually very little unless drink had killed him, and, if not, all that remained had been ravaged by the disease. Finally, an Episcopal cleric in Minneapolis, Vernon Johnson, created a process called "intervention." A group of friends gathered with and around the alcoholic and "raised the bottom." They made it clear that immediate and total change was needed. Change effected through support and a program of therapy and recovery, involved stopping drinking, right now. If this did not happen, then there would be a cost. Those who intervened determined the exact cost, but it often involved loss of job and the withholding of family and personal contact. Love was the necessary pre-condition, but it was "tough love."

Intervention is demanding; the stakes are high. Robert Hall, the former Episcopal Bishop of Virginia, led many such interventions after his own life was saved by an intervention. Bishop Hall often said that not to intervene on behalf of an alcoholic was like walking by a burning building where you knew a person was caught and would be burned alive if you did not do something, but still, you just kept right on walking. Once aware of the situation, to do nothing to save the alcoholic is to consign that person to certain death—even if by slow degrees.

A similar need exists for a person at midlife who comes to the point when all that really matters is just putting in hours until retirement. When this happens, and it does again and again, an intervention may be undertaken to open the eyes of one who needs and deserves a new career. Members of the family or colleagues, together with the employer, should act together to show the way to new opportunity. When a person at age fifty or beyond is settling for too little—just sitting it out until the pension kicks in—the time has come for NEW LIFE. If you know and care for such a person, the obligation is clear.

Most people prefer not to change. When it comes to our own life, we are by nature conservative. "The devil you know is better than the devil you don't know." Changing, moving growing are threatening and unsettling and unwelcome. Those engaged with NEW LIFE must be willing to face this reality and compel the person for whom they care to move forward.

~

Alice began teaching first grade in Seattle thirty-three years ago. She is excellent at what she does and always has been. Well trained, thoughtful, intelligent, attractive, she gives her very best every day. There have just been too many days doing exactly the same thing, year after year.

The children and their parents, especially the mothers, change each year. Alice is a little rigid, but all agree that she does her job well. All, that is, until recently. The Headmaster is not sure if the mothers who now make appointments to come and talk with him about Alice are just representative of the new breed—consumers who expect to receive full value for each dollar paid—or do they really have something.

Each of the three "Alice" conversations he has had with a mother has been similar. The mother begins with praise, telling the Headmaster how much Jim or Jane has learned under Alice's tutelage. Then the tone of the conversation shifts, and there is a litany, a laundry list, of complaints. The words "frozen" "tired," "sterile," "prissy," are the themes. There is the suggestion, that it's time for Alice to go. During the last conversation the Headmaster asked, "So what do you have in mind? Are you suggesting that I fire Alice?"

"Oh, no, no, no, for heaven's sake no," was the reply. "Who could imagine Country Day without Miss Stokes? Alice is an institution. It's just that I'm not sure I'm going to keep my younger one here in school if Alice is going to continue teaching First Grade." That was, as they say, the bottom line.

What was to be done? Something, for sure. Fifteen years stood between Alice and retirement. She couldn't go on that long. She just couldn't. The Headmaster decided to have a little talk with Alice. Nothing confrontational, just a little chat.

It didn't go very well. In fact it never got off the ground. "Everything is fine, thank you," Alice kept saying. "Just fine." When she left the office, the Headmaster felt empty, drained, and a little heartbroken. Alice was so professional, able, dedicated; but Alice had lost her drive.

Meanwhile the signs that it was time for a change became ever more evident. The Headmaster could not help but hear snide remarks, sentences that trailed off without an ending, their meaning abundantly clear. It was serious enough to discuss with the Chair of the Board.

After that conversation, the next step was to gather the Headmaster and the Chair of the Board with some of Alice's best friends and chart a course. It was during that conversation that all learned that Alice spent her weekends volunteering at Children's Hospital. Alice lived alone in her mother's house where the two women had lived together until the mother's death five years ago. Socially poised in all of her professional relationships, it was clear that Alice had few friends and interests outside of school, save for her work at Children's.

The Chair of the Board, George Sparks, knew that one of his colleagues was on the Board at Children's and through that contact, made an appointment with the hospital administrator. This man not only knew of Alice's work at the hospital but lighted up at the mention of her name. George took the plunge, "Would there be a job for Alice at Children's?"

"Job!" replied the administrator. "Nothing would please me and the volunteer staff more. We need a person now to direct the entire volunteer program."

The rest, as they say, is history. Alice Stokes has worked for the last decade at Children's Hospital.

~

Motivation is the first impediment to NEW LIFE. It may be the most frequent, but the second, depression, may be even more crippling.

The diminishment of job satisfaction and fulfillment, and, even worse, the loss of job, will inevitably result in depression. Once depression is present, immobility results.

~

Shortly after mid-day on the opening day of school about halfway through my tenure as headmaster, I had just taken the day's mail home to our house, a hundred yards from my office, when the phone rang. It was the Dean. All he said was, "Get over here. It's Sam. He's in my office."

Sam was the senior member of the faculty who'd been working at the school for well more than thirty years. He worked year-round, for he ran the summer program. He embodied the tradition of the place, was genuinely loved by all who knew him, but he'd been around too long. Only I didn't see that because I needed him too much, not alone for what he did, but for who he was—a symbol and a model.

When I entered the Dean's Office, Sam was sitting in the corner, looking much like himself, but he said nothing, nothing at all. It was clear that he needed help, medical help. He was at the end of his rope. But it was more than that. He was paralyzed, almost literally. We sat together for a while, and then I asked, "Who's your doctor?" He told me. "Here," I said, getting up and moving the phone across the desk next to where Sam was sitting, "Here's the phone. Call him. Call your doctor. I'll take you to see him." Sam didn't move. I repeated myself. Still he didn't move. He couldn't move. So I called the doctor. He was unavailable. I called my own doctor. "Bring Sam to me," he ordered. "I'll be at the hospital." I did as I was told.

All turned out well. But it took many weeks, much good treatment, and a great deal of care and love. I learned something I should have known. When depression strikes, it makes a person immobile, unable to act, even to reach across a desk and pick up a telephone. He can do virtually nothing by himself to help himself. Others have to act for him. It's not easy, but it is necessary.

~

Persons most in need of NEW LIFE will often be depressed. Either at the end of their rope, without hope or expectation, or, even, perhaps, because they have been fired. Desperate, but first and foremost, depressed. One is well advised, therefore, to try and act, to intervene, before depression is present. Once it is, the situation is no less desperate but even more difficult. Still, something must be done. Intervention is now far more necessary. Yet effecting it will be more demanding, even intrusive, but the situation will not solve itself. It will not go away, all by itself, in time. Someone has to move in and make it happen.

~

And when one does this, it will cost money. That's the way of the world. Often, the person needing help will have no money, or money will be in short supply. Without a job, in fear of losing a job, resources stretched, there is not money available.

This is why outplacement firms—those engaged in finding positions for persons who have been fired—will deal only with companies as clients. They work with individuals but on the behalf of the company for whom the person was formerly employed. The corporation, not the individual, pays the outplacement firm, for the individual has meager and limited resources.

Finances are a third impediment to NEW LIFE.

Finances include more than merely the lack of sufficient and readily available financial support to undertake a process of career change. If I leave this job, how do I support myself in the interim before my next job starts? Or, if I now have a job with a secure pension plan and medical insurance and other benefits, why in the world would I put these in jeopardy by looking for new employment? It makes no sense. I better just hang on, which is precisely what I do, shackled by my own understanding of my financial situation.

Time and time again one will hear testimony of the freedom and joy secured by clearing this hurdle and striking out in a new direction. The perceived problems have a way of falling into place and solving themselves,

but before they have ever been encountered—
only imagined, and at a distance—they appear
insolvable and insurmountable.

~

For his first eighteen years after college Peter
pursued a very credible career as an advertising executive. Quick repartee, engaging and
personable, he was well suited to the work. He
became more than successful, close to brilliant and so financially successful that there
was more than enough money invested to
educate their three sons.

It was then that he began to think of other
possibilities, different career directions. What
had he most loved throughout his life? Surely
not advertising. That was merely a way to get
from Point A to Point B, and he'd made that
transition. Advertising had served him well,
but enough was enough.

More and more Peter found himself
dreaming about the days when he was in college, when he read and wrote about F. Scott
Fitzgerald and played a little football. Those
were the days. One thing led to another, and

soon on many afternoons he found himself watching football practice at the high school down the street from their house. The next thing he knew, he'd found time enough to work with the JV football team. One conversation led to another, until Peter wound up talking with the Principal about teaching and coaching, full-time. He started the following September.

It was great, better than great, for ten, then fifteen years before the air came out of Peter's balloon. He wandered around most of the day, left school whenever possible, gave no thought to his teaching and graded papers indifferently.

Sixty years old and tired of the whole thing, he still needed the money, at least some of it, as well as medical coverage and the full pension. Then it happened. The Principal called him in, said he saw the whole thing clearly, offered him an early retirement package—25% salary and full benefits until his pension started in five years. He couldn't believe his ears, but he took it.

The following week he began training as a docent at the art museum and helping out at the retirement home and spent the rest of his time painting with oils.

~

The impediments—motivation, depression, finances—are real, very real. But each and every one of them may be resolved. The illustrations here are only illustrations, indicative of some of the ways in which these matters may be laid to rest. There are many others. Each situation is different from every other. The point is this: there are answers.

NEW LIFE awaits each one of us.

CHAPTER SEVEN

Continuity and Change: Case Studies

Fortunate enough to have been married for fifty years to the person who was my first and only love, I bear testimony to the value of life-long marriage. The most thrilling thing about it is that each day is better and better. We have known heartache, loss and disappointment, but we have encountered these together, making them tolerable and memorable.

Quite aside from the bitter, we have known fulfillment beyond measure; the daily excitement of sharing children, grandchildren, interests, convictions, common and divergent thoughts and insights. Each day brings gratitude and hope, amazed to be so fortunate, excited to be alive, to share another day.

The most interesting challenge we now face, as we stop being employed and start our own business, is should we move or stay in the city where we have lived for a decade. We have moved twelve times expressing two professions in different ways and different locations, seeking different ways to be refreshed and renewed.

We ask, "How shall we do it the next time?" We have no desire to stop work. Work has bound us together through fifty years. Whether the pursuit of each day has kept us physically apart or drawn us together, we have always been united, philosophically and theologically, in common understanding and common passion to offer ourselves to others and to one another. This has made our life together ever more exciting. So we believe it should continue.

While each one of us is constantly tempted to believe and to act as if "It's all about me," this is not the case. There are many different ways to understand and approach the life each of us has been given, but if the central theme is continuity, then through it all, there is the necessity for change, refreshment, renewal.

This is the rhythm of NEW LIFE.

What follows are vignettes, case studies, short stories describing two different persons, who sought and found new life. Each story is instructive and taken together they form a pattern that will be summarized in Chapter Eight, a pattern of relevance and purpose that will reveal a new expression for your new life.

~

Well past his fiftieth birthday, Sean Smith still looked like the innocent young boy who had showed up with 108 others as new students in the ninth grade at Hartshorne School. Almost shy, but with a disarming smile and ready response, Sean had grown up in what he always described as an average middle-class family in Huntington, West Virginia. There was never anything average about Sean; his performance during those four high school years included highest honors, varsity basketball, three times class president. His nature was to lead, but whenever he did so, he did not fail to include others. His native instinct was always to move forward and to make a difference, but to do so Sean always realized it was essential to help others to move with him.

Long before his senior year, there was only one college, but when Sean arrived at Indiana University an unexpected thing happened. He let go of everything that had once seemed important, dropped out of the world, he had known, moved to Indianapolis and virtually disappeared. He formed a rock band, became a drug addict, was excused from college. He spent his time driving a taxi, growing his hair down to his waist, playing in the band, doing drugs.

As it turned out, these five years were part of Sean's transition. Whether it was merely the passing of time or a failed marriage, he came to himself, re-enrolled in college, finished with straight A's and graduated at age twenty-seven. Business school was a breeze. Sean was on to Wall Street, arriving in the mid-80s.

At the end of ten years he had made his first fortune, considered retiring and did. After only three months, he knew this was not for him, and he returned to the world of finance, where he kept making more and more money. When enough was more than enough, he bailed out—for good. Sean knew how much he had; normal people found it impossible to conceive.

What to do?

He helped his wife start her own publishing house. The two of them built a new expansive, dream house they named Fairhaven. His brother, Tom, wanted Sean to help him start his own construction business back in Huntington. Sean became active on the board of a hospital and an inner-city homeless shelter, was attentive to his children now away in boarding school, writing and visiting them, making trips to see their games. He joined a choral group, gave up golf, took flying lessons, even bought an airplane, tried collecting old flint glass and Civil War daguerreotypes. His wife hosted the party of his and every lifetime when he turned fifty. No one had ever attended anything like it.

The only problem was that none of this really worked. "What is it?" he asked himself, daily, hourly. "How can I find the one thing that I really want to do?" Then it came to him, how to find the answer. He would gather in one place and at one time the five people who knew him best: Susan, his wife; Chuck, his closest friend from school; Charlene his executive assistant during his years on Wall Street; Dan, the other senior partner from their old firm; Paul, who lived next door and sang with Sean in the choral group.

Sean proposed a house party weekend at their new house. Spouses were welcome, but the weekend was all about Sean. The invitation carefully created and presented. His letter enclosed a one page resume of the facts of his life and a longer, well-written, narrative resume that included facts, figures, accomplishments and honors, all considerable. The letter read:

"As you know, I am at a turning point. There is no need for me to do anything and every reason to identify and undertake what should be the most important contribution that remains for me to offer a world too full of takers—like me—and not many givers of the kind I should become.

"Towards this end I write to make the most important single request I have ever made. You are a trusted and good friend. Your help is essential.

"My life has been more than good, but it is

scarcely over. What do I do next? My available options are many, but at this moment none hits me as the one that is best for me. This is why I turn to you and ask you to spend a weekend with Susie and me here at our house, Fairhaven. Your task: to determine what is the best future for me at this time.

"This is very self-serving, and I apologize, but I only ask because you know me so well. You are one of five good friends to whom I turn, friends *who know me and know what I know and can do.* Working together your insights will create new energy.

"Once this letter is in your hands, I shall be in touch to confirm the time, date and final arrangements. It is essential that each of you be present and with me for the entire weekend. It will change my life and lay the sure foundation for my future and our friendship.

"Many, many thanks. I look forward to our time together."

Everyone accepted. Who could not? The weekend included time for good food, conversation, tennis and swimming, but there were structured, formal conversations on the first evening, after dinner; for the entire following morning, after breakfast; throughout dinner on the second evening; and after breakfast on the final morning. Before lunch there was conclusion and consensus. Both came as a surprise.

Through all those hours of conversation and deliberation, this was most clear: Sean's life had been changed, launched, set on a new course when he went away to boarding school. Although he was now active as a trustee, planner and benefactor for his own school, Sean was especially equipped thanks to his intelligence, insight and resources to undertake an effort to change the lives of many heretofore unknown younger persons all around the United States. The opportunity that had been afforded to Sean could be offered many times over and would be thanks to Sean's initiative, organization and resources.

Sean established and ran a national talent search organization that identified, supported, educated and launched young people of middle school age. Beginning in five schools in five cities, it expanded into seven, then twelve, then twenty schools and cities, finding children of promise in disadvantaged circumstances, providing for their education locally or at independent schools.

Sean changed the lives of first hundreds and then thousands of students.

~

Anne Cartwright, tall, willowy, self-assured, was born into a Providence Rhode Island family of privilege and position. Bloodlines, heritage, breeding, wealth were all simply the way things were. More than intelligent and superbly educated, she excelled at both her school and college, institutions that some believed were the best in the country.

Then she made a disastrous marriage. Despite all her efforts at denial, its ill effects could not be minimized. There was no question that John was able and successful, but he was also duplicitous, unreliable, unfaithful and largely absent from their family life. The children lacked any direction and purpose, Anne was alone most waking hours and went to bed each night, bereft, only to toss and turn, wonder and worry.

She had learned from her mother and father to be faithful, subservient, decent and Godly, and she would not forsake her marriage vows, although sometimes this was all she wanted to do. Anne continued to persevere against all odds until the night when John was in the worst of all his drunken rages and beat her so badly that she spent a week in the hospital. Anne had talked extensively with her lawyer before she was released from the hospital; she and John never lived in the same house again.

Age forty-seven, Anne struggled to believe that her life had not been a complete waste. There were the two children, boy and girl, but neither had time or use for mother. Driven to the very limits of her resources, Anne did the most radical thing of her life: she took a job.

As a faithful, even obedient, socially conscious upper-class woman, Anne had volunteered at a museum and a hospital and served as a Trustee of her children's school. She had achieved considerable success as a fund-raiser for the school, planned and effected campaigns, small and nearly large. Her knowledge and connections were considerable. Her bright idea was to apply for a job as Director of Development at another, nearby independent school. The job was offered, and she took it.

Anne, always energetic, was most herself when organizing events and people. Her work met with success. Better still, she really enjoyed it, and the salary provided a new sense of self worth. Sometimes she wondered if she would have found this career if John had not gotten so drunk that night and beaten her so badly.

After Anne completed directing a capital campaign, she began to wonder more and more if she had not completed the learning curve in this job. It was then, out of the blue, that she received a call from the hospital across town. "We'd welcome the opportunity to talk with you." She agreed that she would welcome that opportunity, too. The hospital offered a bigger, better job than the one she held. Anne fulfilled her contract with the school and put on a new hat. More money, more challenge, more occasions to learn and to grow.

She did both, did them both so well that three years later she was offered a position with a large, nation-wide consulting firm to support the fund-raising needs of different non-profits. The clients to whom she was assigned were in diverse, different and interesting places around the country. She traveled extensively, returning home each weekend. The more she did this work, the more she liked it, and the more she knew she wanted to establish her own consulting firm: Cartwright & Associates.

She did just that.

~

Two quite different persons each faced with the opportunity and the challenge to find a new life at midlife. Each a unique individual who embodies a pattern, a pathway found in many others. You may find yourself in one of these persons, or you may hear echoes, loud or faint, of whom you may become. If so, the chances are very strong you need to discover a new career. NEW LIFE is for you.

CHAPTER EIGHT

Making It Happen for You

Whatever the pattern your professional life has followed, no doubt it has evolved as it should. Choices were offered; you made them. One choice led on to another. There is no road back, but obviously there is a road ahead. That road ahead offers different alternatives that have the possibility to fulfill in a number of different ways the choices you have already made.

When you arrive at midlife, the time has come to exercise new choices and to fulfill new opportunities. The chances are that you will need help to make this happen. It will not happen all by itself.

What these new directions, these changes are and what will be required to make them happen for you are contained—often hidden—within the interactions and the people that have touched, changed and directed you throughout your life. These persons and events continue to be present and active in your life, but you need to have the eyes to see, the ears to hear, and the heart to understand.

Once you have these—eyes, ears, heart—open, active and operative, then it will be necessary to act. You need to use your own very important insights. How do you do this?

Not all by yourself. Motivation to undertake a new career direction does not strike when you wall yourself off from the world, its people, its processes and its pressures. What this book describes and makes available to you takes place through personal interaction at many levels. This interaction is happening to you all the time, whether you are aware of it or not, most often when you are not aware at all. This means that opportunities are being created and made available to you constantly, but you have to take action and involve others to access them. You have to hear the knock and open the door. You will see the opportunity that awaits you.

But you will have to hear, see, understand, or otherwise that person, that agency of change, that possible new direction in your life, will go away.

Let us return to Charles Allen, whom we met in Chapter 1. Charles, who is now well past sixty, is required to seek a new career opportunity, for the one he has so ably filled for more than twenty years has been snatched from him. What might he have done, should he have done, sometime in the past before his current change was required?

What would have happened if ten years ago a new direction had been recommended to him? This is what would have happened.

If ten years ago, some one had said, "Charles, you'd better start looking now, while all your options are open. When the day comes, for it surely will, when you *are forced* to make such a move, your choices will be far more limited than if you take the initiative now."

If someone had had the audacity and the wisdom to state such a judgment, Charles would have laughed or been enraged or become sarcastic. It's very similar to the attitude of the average sixteen-year-old who does not believe—not really and truly—that he will ever die. He thinks he's immortal, but he isn't. Just as surely, you and I and Charles— all of us—are going to need a new career direction. If not tomorrow, then sometime in the not-so-distant future.

Most often our hopes and plans for the future direction of our career happen through fantasy; imagination helps shape, then long for, and find and achieve our next career. Sometimes that's exactly what happens, but it does not happen that way as often as we hope.

Far more often this kind of thinking and planning and maneuvering that will shape our future careers is done by others on our behalf. In every field of endeavor there are wise, perceptive persons who are consulted, asked to name prospective candidates for significant positions, job opportunities. These persons do not operate in a vacuum and are available when asked by those interested in filling vacant positions. These persons are available to you. Who are they? You can name them, seek them out, find them, encourage them to work on your behalf. Only the way in which you may and should do so is quite different from what you are may think.

Some of these persons set themselves up as professional "movers and shakers," while, for others, it is a casual avocation. In either case such people are available to you if you seek them out and are open to them.

Charles Allen has old friends, persons he has known literally for a lifetime who know him and his talents well. So, too, he has professional colleagues, persons for whom and with whom he has worked, as well as persons who have worked for him. When those friendships and relationships have been positive, and for the most part they have been, then there is no reason why these people would not be thrilled to be available to Charles as a resource to support and help him as he plots his next professional move.

There are two impediments in the case of Charles Allen. The first is motivation, and it exists for virtually all people. Why fix it if it's not broken? Why look around to change when everything is fine?

Why? Because you have to, and if you do not, the time will come when you hear the words, "We've decided to go in a different direction. It's time to make a change."

The second impediment is that Charles has arrived at the place and in the job that has been his dream. He has achieved everything he hoped would be possible; therefore, why even think of what's next? Why? This is precisely the right time to begin to frame your answer to "What's next?" just as did those persons with whom I sat on the lawn preparing to leave headmastering. They were only beginning, and in that moment they thought about their future.

This may not appear to happen frequently, but at some level it happens to everyone, and when it does, we say to ourselves, If you've arrived on the top of your chosen heap and can see for miles in every direction, sooner or later someone is going to come along and knock you off that perch.

So what should Charles have done a decade ago? His best friend, his conscience or his counselor might have said this:

"Charles. Let's just pretend, pretend that you're not going to continue just as you are indefinitely. There is nothing else in this world that you want to do more, but what if? What if there were? What if you had to make a change, find a new direction? What would you most want to do?"

Charles would reply, "I have no idea. There's nothing else that I want to do. Nothing at all."

And then his friend, conscience or counselor would say, "I understand. I understand perfectly. But everyone should always know what is going to happen next. Every single person needs to have a Plan B, an alternate course, to pursue when Plan A—what you are doing now—comes to an end, for surely it must and it will.

"How can you and I together arrive at a Plan B—what's next? Let me tell you. Let's gather three or four or five of the most important people in your life, people who not only know you, but the people who know what you know and know what you do—your professional skills, insights and abilities. Let me suggest whom we might choose.

❧ "First, let's choose Ralph. You met him first when you were ten. You've not only been friends ever since, but you have a great deal in common, speak to each other, once a week.

🎕 "Second, let's choose Jim. He was the best boss you have ever had. You worked together with him for more than a decade, and your work with him was superb. He knows you well, keeps in touch, values everything you do.

🎕 "Third, we should ask Hank. He's been a close professional colleague for twenty-five years. I can not accurately list all the many projects you have undertaken together.

🎕 "So, this means that we assemble a group of five people: you, me, Ralph, Jim and Hank. Let me contact those three and explain to them what we have in mind, and then let us get together for a good three-hour period when our only focus is you, your abilities, what the future could hold. You will be present as an observer. I want you to hear but not speak unless given permission. This will not be easy for you, but it will also be interesting.

🎕 "We'll go round the room. I'll moderate. You'll listen. Ralph, Jim and Hank will tell us all everything they can remember about how they know you, when and in what contexts. They will describe in some detail what you do best. Weaknesses may be mentioned, perhaps, but we are most interested in strengths. Once they have enumerated your strengths, then I shall ask them to interact with one another weaving those strengths together in new and different ways. How can they, as your friends, advocates and supporters see you in new and different environments, facing new and different challenges— the kinds of things that the future holds for you which may have never, ever, even have occurred to you.

"That's just the beginning of what I have in mind. It's only an exercise. But it's about real life, and the stakes are high. What do you think?"

Most likely, Charles would not know what to say. The idea, your proposal, is all too new, completely unknown, and more than a little threatening. The appeal is that it's all about him. It's asking him to give three hours to spend with you and three very close friends as the complete center of attention. A heady invitation. He'd be very tempted, with a few additional words of encouragement, to accept.

And what would be the result? NEW LIFE.

How will that come about? Why should this particular group of people think of something that Charles would not have thought of all by himself?

Why? These people have been brought together with the precise purpose to envision Charles's future in a new way not yet imagined. They will rise to the occasion.

How do I know this? It has happened for me, not once but several times, when other persons, known and unknown, acted on my behalf when seeking just the right person for a specific position. More than once these people—a different group in each case—went through all the necessary and accepted, the normal, steps and motions to fill a particular job with just the right, normal, acceptable person. But nothing happened. There was no right answer, the "right" person did not appear. There was no result.

So, they looked at one another, and said in so many words: "Wipe the slate clean. Start all over. Whom do you know who could best do this job?"

There is no reason, no reason at all why that system can not be turned on its head and made to work for you to help you find a new career direction. The point is that NEW LIFE *is* beyond belief. And it's all about you. And it can and will work.

Herb Gardner's classic play "A Thousand Clowns" is, among other things, about a job search, an unsuccessful job search. The text, the mantra, that the central figure of the play keeps repeating is that we have to live in the available world. He wants to believe that he cannot construct solutions that do not exist.

But the fact is that we can create those solutions, only not all by ourselves. We are not put on this earth to live alone but in community with others. Those others will help us by searching for, finding, creating those new solutions that will then become available.

NEW LIFE is a process that will help you seek, find and create the solutions that are best for you.

It's all about you. But the process that is NEW LIFE can not be attempted alone, not in isolation, which is why, "We're here for you."

The Promise of a New Beginning

The ten-year-old daughter of a former student died after a long, agonizing bout with cancer. Two of the father's classmates wrote me nearly identical emails that said, "I cannot even imagine his pain."

Nor can I. We are the parents of three daughters, now grown, with children of their own. Who can even imagine the pain at the loss of such promise? No one.

Except it happens. It happens to each of us. Not in that precise way, but each of us has:

ℰ lost the dream job of a lifetime because it was never offered, or

- been forced to leave a job before it was finished, or

- stood at the graveside of a parent or sibling, knowing we had not said it all, not what we could have said, should have said, or

- driven into the sunset wondering where we were going or why, or

- opened our eyes and closed them, wishing the day would never begin, or

- realized that some day we shall have to say goodbye to the one person who matters most, and we know, really know, that we just can never do that.

This book has only dealt with one significant part of your life: finding a new career direction at midlife and beyond. What this book wants to tell you, convince you of, is that the challenge of a new direction at midlife is an absolute essential for each and every person. You may avoid this reality, you may deny it, but this will not change the fact that it is a necessity. So why not face it?

Death happens. You will either die, internally, on the job, or you will be forced out.

The alternative is to take the initiative. That's what NEW LIFE is all about—taking the initiative. Why? Two reasons.

First, you must. You really have no other choice.

Second, when you do, there is the inevitable promise of a new beginning.

The end is never the end.

NEW LIFE responds to two different possibilities. Either you are aware, you did notice and you want to take steps now to prevent becoming empty. It is time for NEW LIFE. Or, you didn't notice, and you are empty. It is the time for NEW LIFE.

A woman was carrying a jar full of meal. While she was walking along a distant road, the handle of the jar broke and the meal spilled behind her along the road. She didn't know it; she hadn't noticed a problem. When she reached her house, she put the jar down and discovered that it was empty.